C000057894

BREWERY TRANSPORT

Arthur Ingram

ROUNDOAK PUBLISHING, NYNEHEAD, WELLINGTON, SOMERSET

First published in 1991 by
Roundoak Publishing (an imprint of Nynehead Books).
Nynehead
Wellington
Somerset
England TA21 0BX

British Library Cataloguing in Publication Data

Ingram, Arthur
   Trucks in Britain: Brewery Transport
   1. Great Britain, Road freight transport services
   I. Title
   388.3'24

ISBN 1-871565-04-9

Design and typesetting by   Printed in Great Britain by
Haight Ashbury Design   **The Amadeus Press**
Stoke Sub Hamdon   **Huddersfield**
Somerset   **West Yorkshire**

This view of Luton brewery, taken in 1955 soon after the acquisition of Flower & Sons by J. W. Green, shows the main part of the brewery buildings as well as three different vehicle types. With everything now lettered as Flowers, the Bedford in the foreground was one of a large number of this make in the fleet used for house deliveries. Immediately behind is one of the few AEC Mammoth Major 80-barrel tanks for bulk deliveries to remote bottling depots, whilst the two Commer artics have the impressive streamlined Carrimore van trailers with the highly unusual sliding roofs for overhead loading.

Ever since the early days of my interest in commercial vehicles, the brewery fleets have held a particular attraction, probably because of the smart turn-out of their vehicles. With a product that has been in constant demand for centuries, it comes as no surprise that brewing companies have notably been wealthy operations, hence their ability to have some of the best vehicles and equipment possible.

To the vehicle enthusiast the great pity is undoubtedly the gradual decline in the number of independent brewing companies in the country. This decline being reflected by the dwindling number of individual fleet liveries, company (and family) names, public houses, and of even more importance to beer drinkers, the wholesale abandonment of local 'brews'.

The practice of amalgamations, take-overs, groupings and any other kind of combinations among brewers is nothing new. It is almost as old as the industry itself, but the brewing giants which have been formed in, say, the last 30-40 years year really spelled the end of a lot of historical individuality from the point of view of us onlookers.

One of my personal regrets is that I never managed to record the vehicles of many of the old brewing companies that have now disappeared, but that just seems part of life. Luckily many photographs do exist of at least some of the older brewery names and vehicles, and I am sure that many others still remain to be discovered.

So, this volume attempts to revive a few memories of names that once graced old vehicles, but it is not an attempt to make any wild claims to do more than scratch the surface of the paintwork which covers many of the gone-with-regret vehicles of yesteryear. But some of the modern names are recorded, because this is a book about brewery vehicles in general, and not an historical survey. By using photographs gleaned from many sources it is hoped that a broad picture emerges of a variety of vehicle types and styles operated by brewers in many parts of the country.

My own experience in the industry probably shows through in the text, and it is hoped that it is not too biased one way or another. Any emphasis about the two companies I worked for is purely coincidental, and can probably be easily spotted by the reader — trouble is that beer tends to get into your veins!

I would like to place on record my grateful thanks to the many companies who have provided photographs, be they vehicle manufacturers, bodybuilders or brewers. Also to those fellow enthusiasts who have helped in the same way, notably Peter Davies, Roger Kenney and particularly Ron Wilkins who put his whole collection at my disposal. Finally I must mention that great historical work, Friedrichs Gazetteer of British Breweries, which contains such a wealth of information on our old brewing companies. **Arthur Ingram**

INTRODUCTION

As one of the staple industries of this country, the brewery companies have usually invested great amounts of time and energy in maintaining fine fleets of vehicles to carry out their deliveries, as well as performing a vital publicity function.

The old brewery companies were renowned for their horses in the early days of road transport, and this state of affairs continued, and in some cases expanded and improved, with the introduction of motor vehicles. They attached great importance to the presentation of their motor fleets, often entering the competitions which were organised to enhance the appearance and condition of motor vehicles in the early days of motor transport, thus continuing what had been established in the horsedrawn era. The current LDOY competitions are the modern counterparts of these old established events.

Traditionally the brewery fleet was made up of British vehicles of good quality, fully equipped and well presented in a rich solid colour with the owners name perhaps in gold leaf for good measure.

Brewery vehicles had to be well built, because beer is heavy, and the strong oak casks were also heavy, the reinforcing metal hoops and chimes particularly wearing on the bodywork. The old draymans leather apron was well used when man-handling casks on deliveries and in cellars, and the vehicles had to be similarly hard wearing, using the best hardwoods with plenty of metal reinforcement at stress or wear points.

Vehicles manufacturers were continually wooing the brewery companies, for their vehicle fleets were a great asset in the sphere of advertising, even though some brewers used to remove the vehicle nameplates as soon as they were delivered!

Some vehicle builders designed vehicles with the brewery fleets in mind, and often built their bodies for them as well. In many instances brewery companies and vehicle builders stayed together for many years because of the mutual trust enjoyed by both parties.

Looking back over the years it is possible to trace examples of particular allegiance by one company for an individual vehicle builder. Of course location played a big part in the arrangements, it would certainly be unusual for a Hampshire brewery to always specify Albion vehicles, and conversely the Dennis and Thornycroft names were rather rarely seen in Scotland. But Leylands were very popular in the North-West, just as one would imagine, and Bedfords and Commers were popular in the Home Counties, although this regional preference disappeared as brewers and transport managers became directed by accountants.

The gradual elimination of home built vehicles has had less impact in the brewery industry than that of road haulage, when imported vehicles are now more frequently seen than ever before. However AWD and ERF are by no means the major

Above: This fine photograph shows the maintenance facility of William Younger & Co in Edinburgh, probably some time during the late 1950s. In the forefront is a Commer service van of 1952 with a Leyland 'Beaver' tractor unit close behind. On the next inspection pit stands a 1954 Austin 'Loadstar' flat, with a Leyland 'Comet' and Austin delivery vehicles over the next two bays, while in the background stands what appears to be a 60 barrel tank.

Latest in the generation of 'urban artics' is the 20 tonne model from AWD, pictured here in the fleet operated by Bass Worthington from the old Mitchell & Butlers Springfield Brewery in Wolverhampton.

vehicle suppliers as yet, and one wonders how long it will be before we see German, Italian and Japanese vehicles carrying the more familiar beer brand names.

Not that all you see is real, for the brewers like other sections of industry are changing more to hiring, leasing and contract operation, rather than buying and maintaining their own fleets. Not that using the vehicles of a professional haulier is anything new, ever since the early days of motor vehicles there have been instances of brewers hiring-in vehicles in preference to running their own. Even the modern term 'dedicated' when applied to a contract of fleet is merely repeating what has gone before — no one was more dedicated to their brewery customers than Thomas Allen Ltd on the Guinness contract or United Service Transport for Bass-Worthington!

To any student of road transport, the fleets operated by brewers have contained more outstanding vehicles in their time. No one can deny the sombre elegance of the old Guinness dark blue with gold lettering, the rich dark green of Watneys or the solid brown of Whitbreads. Of course there were dozens more, each bearing the unmistakable mark of its owners and with a richness that reflected the established quality of the beers it carried.

Unfortunately there appeared to be a distinct falling-off of standards during that era of take-overs and amalgamations, which blighted the British brewing industry during the last 30 years or so. Many of the old familiar liveries were varied or changed completely together with the adoption of modern logos or contrived trademarks. Often the rich dark colours gave way to modern pastel shades, or worse still the vehicles appeared with little form of identification, save perhaps for a small fleet number in white.

So many of the old names disappeared altogether. No sooner was a merger or take-over announced, than the brewery was closed down, the bottling stores reclassified as distribution depots and the fleet sold off and replaced with the new standard designs.

Luckily the trend seems to be running out of steam. We are now treated to newly-created trading names with vehicles swamped in names of new imported beers. There are probably more varieties of lager nowadays than there were breweries in 1950! But at least the fleets seem to be improving and the liveries of some are quite attractive if rather bright — they look good when they're new but will they keep them clean?

The major part of any brewery fleet is that which is used to carry out deliveries to its retail customers, such as the public houses, clubs and off-licences. As with most things, the lines of demarcation become blurred on occasions and with such deliveries as other breweries or giant supermarket warehouses, the delivery vehicle can be as large as the maximum capacity outfit of the company.

Usually, however, local delivery vehicles tend to be at the smaller end of gross vehicle weights with payloads from about 1 tonne to 10 tonnes. At one time these vehicles were all of the rigid type, but over the years the articulated layout has been tried with varying degrees of success.

Body style has also undergone some major changes. It seems that fleets have gone through phases of using a plain flat body, a flat with chains or bars, a normal dropside type or a flat with part fixed slatted sides with hinged sections for load access.

Another style was the loose tilt over a central bar, or the slatted side with a fixed roof over. Yet another was the boarded tilt where waterproofed canvas was stretched over a close-boarded van type body, and a further variation was the completely enclosed van with doors, although this was usually reserved for the high priced items such as wines and spirits.

In more recent years there have been replaceable bodies, demountable bodies, curtainsides and vehicles equipped with miniature fork trucks and lorry-mounted cranes as aids to easier and safer load-handling. In this latter respect the height of the load platform has attracted much attention, it varying from about 4 feet down to about a metric foot. Originally the loading height was determined by having the load platform above the wheels and axles of the carrying vehicle, a height which had been established earlier by horsedrawn transport and then the railways.

Having the vehicle floor at chest level was quite OK when beer was contained in casks which were easy to handle when on the roll, and could be slid down the barrel skid to ground level before being lowered down the cellar skid into the public house. There was the problem of getting the casks back out of the cellar and on to the vehicle however, but at least they were empty!

With the gradual introduction of bottled beer the handling problems changed, and new methods had to be introduced as an aid to safe and economic handling, both at the vehicle and into

Above: It was in 1906 that the photographer found this Foden overtype steam wagon of Seabrooke & Sons Ltd from Grays, delivering to a public house in Southend-on-Sea. With half the vehicle length taken up by the boiler, engine and crew quarters, the stout rear axle is placed centrally under the load carrying portion. The body itself is a robust frame affair with hinged side sections and the complete tail-gate hinges down to ground level to give access to the load. The two small boys find the photographer more interesting than either the steam wagon of the repairs going on at the roadside, while those two enormous gas lamps outside the public house must have acted like beacons to thirsty travellers of the time.

the customers premises. At the depot the crates were brought close to, or in some circumstances, actually on to the vehicle, from where they could be stacked by hand. In smaller establishments the stacks of crates might be handled by a sack truck.

At the delivery point the bottled beer crates could perhaps be handed off one at a time, stacked on the ground and then trucked into the storage if on ground level. For cellar deliveries it might be a case of sliding the crates down a plank and then stacking by hand. If the delivery had to be made upstairs, then that really was another story!

Palletisation of bottled beer helped at the loading point but was of no consequence at the delivery end, particularly if the beer was loaded by type. This meant that there was a fair amount of sorting to be done on the vehicle as the delivery round progressed.

It was because of the need for the delivery crew (usually two) to have to continually reach up and down at each unloading point, that prompted so much agitation to get loading heights reduced. Otherwise there was always the plea for an extra crew member to help out!

Brewery companies tried vainly to achieve lower platforms on vehicles by a variety of means which included smaller vehicles, which because of smaller diameter wheels had lower body floors, but this meant using more vehicle journeys for a given tonnage.

Another trend was to mount the body cross-members directly onto the chassis member and so save a few inches, but then the wheels had no room to bounce, so wheel arches had to be provided for the back wheels — at a height greater than the rest of the floor!

To reduce the wheel and tyres size would have helped, but

The brewers were into steam haulage at an early stage, and they were equally as swift at trying the faltering early heavy motor lorries. A very early example is this vehicle operated by Huggins & Co of the Lion Brewery in Broad Street in central London. It is a German-built Daimler, distributed in this country by G. F. Milnes & Co and called Milnes-Daimler probably in order to sound slightly less Teutonic. It has shaft drive to toothed ring gear on the inside of the rear wheels, and the rear axle is located by those massive wooden torque-reaction bars. The mud-encrusted hand brake working on the rear wheel tread is worthy of note, as is the body which has no floor — merely bearers to carry the barrels making up the load.

then the loading capacity of the vehicle was reduced accordingly. Some brewers attempted to compensate for this by adding another axle — first at the rear and at a later date by using the twin steer axle layout. For a short while a couple of brewers even tried the rigid four axle layout in order to maintain the low height/capacity balance.

Yet another idea was to try front wheel drive, for this could allow a full-sized, adequate-capacity front drive and steer axle, and by using two rear axles with wheels and tyres of diminished size, the vehicle floor could be reasonably low. Unfortunately front steer/drive axles are expensive and usually result in a reduction in turning ability — a possibly unacceptable compromise.

At least one brewer tried out the idea of using a fully low-loading articulated trailer for local deliveries which provided the draymen with a floor line hardly above the level of the kerb! Yet this was not that successful, for with hand unloading it was almost as wearing to keep bending down as it was to reach upwards!

The problems of load security are almost as old as the variety of body styles, this ranging from a sheet and ropes through to a complete box van. Most local delivery loads have to be sorted or moved, however slightly, sometimes during the delivery round, and this can lead to problems with load movement. Many of the very earliest of specially-built brewery vehicles had a very strong slatted body of hardwood carried up to the height of the vehicle cab. This was ideal for a mixed load which had to be sorted along the way, but they rarely appear to have been loaded to full capacity.

The modern trend has been to use the whole of the vehicle floor and even to stack the load two metres high in order to obtain full capacity. So that accessibility to the load is maintained, the curtainsider type has proved to be most useful in this respect, especially the later designs which incorporate reinforcement and tensioning of the curtain.

Below: This early photograph shows three Berna vehicles carrying banners displaying the Ind Coope & Co name, although they are obviously manufacturers or dealers demonstration vehicles. The date is probably around 1910, and the location Avonmore Road, Kensington, which was the address of the British distributors for the marque. The numbers 6, 8 and 9 on the vehicles are their identification in the Heavy Vehicle Trials of the period, and it could well be that they were carrying the liquid refreshment for both participants and officials!

Left: Although the brewers were renowned for their modern thinking, and many of them turned to motor vehicles very early in the century, this was not the brewery transport of the day. This unusual 1908 rear engined Dennis tractor had been ordered by South African Railways, and Dennis Brothers used this old steam wagon drawbar trailer loaded with hogsheads from the local Friary, Holroyd & Healy's Breweries, as a load test before sending the tractor on its way.

Below: Local Delivery -1912 Style. This fine period photograph shows a 4-ton Milnes Daimler in service with Messrs Style & Winch Ltd of Maidstone. Although undoubtedly an official photograph, the load appears random enough to be genuine, save for the fact that the kilderkin casks on the roll do not appear to be secured in any way, perhaps they had been put up there in order to make the load appear larger. Although the crew protection is almost non-existent, a nice touch is the way the load stabilisers at the front of the body are carried up to the roof line, which gives a tidy appearance.

Right: The Tadcaster Tower Brewery Co. Ltd were the operators of this unusual steam wagon which has all the appearance of being a petrol engined lorry. Built by the Sheppee Motor and Engineering Co of York, which was only some 30 miles from Tadcaster, the vehicle boasted a liquid fuel boiler situated under the bonnet and centrally-mounted underfloor engine. The front mounted 'radiator' is in fact a steam condenser and the driver sat over the water tank. It would appear to be used for the internal transport of sacks of malt in this 1914 photograph.

Below: The Lancashire Steam Motor Company with premises at Leyland, were well placed to handle the demand for heavy vehicles for the brewing industry of Lancashire. Nearby Preston could boast literally dozens of small brewers during the last 100 years or so, so there has been no shortage of customers in this part of the country. This 1908 machine was destined for the fleet of Daniel Thwaites & Co Ltd of Blackburn and is seen loaded with test weights ready for a test run and complete with the driver's bicycle in case he needs to ride back to the factory for assistance!

Above: Although electric vehicles are virtually silent in operation, the old GV Electric lorries operated by Meux & Co announced their arrival by the 'whirr' of their open chain drive. Some of the last survivors of heavy electrics for road use, they dated from the 1920s, that period when large electrics were vying with the petrol vehicle as replacements for the diminishing fleets of horsed transport. As some were acquired second-hand, the Meux GVs were a motley collection, some having fixed sides and some slatted sides, they being originally fitted with tilt covers. Similarly, some retained the original open-fronted cabs whilst others had the luxury of a windscreen. Most had no headlights, probably in order to conserve the batteries!

Below: An old sepia print which bears the stamp of E. A. Turner who photographed quite a number of vehicles in the street in the early days of motor transport. This lovely old Leyland was in service with Brandons Brewery of Putney when photographed on a delivery in 1911. The two period draymen have paused from unloading those crates of flagons from the 35hp 70-cwt capacity vehicle, but the front dropside seems to have been detached for some reason. The huge illuminated roof sign has three ventilators fitted, for it was lit by paraffin lamps which were tended by the driver!

Right: Many old brewery companies liked to advertise their products as having certain qualities which were beneficial to the drinkers. In the early days it was the heavy types of beer and stout that were supposed to contain additives for the greatest benefits, with milk stout and oatmeal stout probably being the most publicised, although the Colchester Brewing Co's 'Oyster Feast' Stout sounds a mouthful! The Burtonwood Brewery Company of Newton-le-Willows was the operators of this 1913 2-ton Pagefield which advertises their 'Silver Buckle' stout and 'Invalid Stout'. The body style is a variation of a very old type used in the north of England, particularly in the Lancashire cotton industry, with a central bar to support a sheet, the edges of which were tied down to the body sides. In this design the stanchions and chains have been added as security for the heavy casks.

Below: Resplendent with its white-wall 40"x8" tyres, this 1920s Leyland GH2 4 tonner was powered by the maker's 4 cylinder 36hp engine, and ample breathing was via the multitude of bonnet louvres, each one carefully coach-lined. The vehicle is lettered in the livery of John Aitchison of Edinburgh but appears to be supplied or operated by A. J. Morrison who was the local agent for Aitchisons beers, or the haulage contractor. The patent reflective headboard is unusual on a brewery vehicle, but the polished wood windscreen surround and mixture of electric headlamps and oil sidelights are typical of the period.

Botton right: Rogers' Ales and Stouts were the products of W. J. Rogers Ltd. of Jacobs Street Brewery, Bristol, who were acquired by H & G Simonds of Reading in 1935. This vehicle is a Hallford with enclosed chain final drive, and the elegant tilt type bodywork was built by the Bristol Tramways and Carriage Company. The vehicle was photographed at the Bristol factory before entering service in 1913, and interestingly was supplied on contract hire to the brewers by Bristol Tramways.

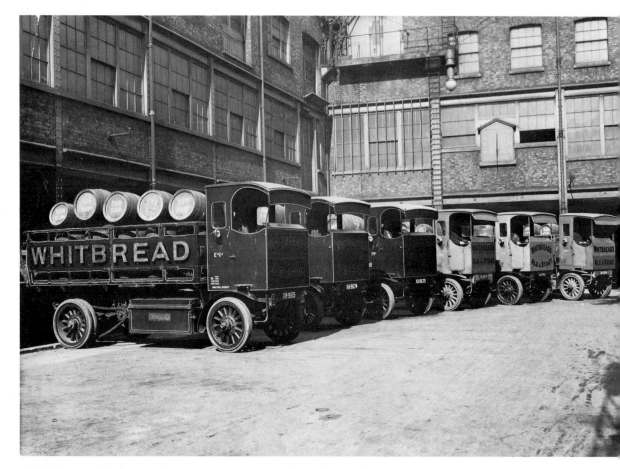

Above: This view of the first six of the GV electric 5 tonners in service with Whitbreads, shows the subtle difference between two different batches delivered to the brewer in the early 1920s. The first three are in the background and appear to be in the old green livery, while the trio in the foreground are in the more familiar chocolate brown with gold lettering. A total of 15 of these electrics operated from the city brewery, and by the mid-1930s they had been converted to pneumatic tyres. Some were fitted with windscreens later in life, and some passed to other brewers in the early post-war years.

Above right: Joseph Johnson (Durham) Ltd were the proprietors of Westoe Brewery in South Shields before 1960 when control passed to Hammond's United Breweries of Bradford. This neat little 1930 Thornycroft is done out in fine style, and the driver must have been very proud of having such a comfortable cab with full doors, drop windows and all electric lighting. The ponderous roof sign was not illuminated, but was of a patent type which relied upon natural daylight being projected through the sign and reflected toward the front.

Right: It seemed only natural to most brewers, that they should obtain their motor lorries locally, just as they had done in the days of horse drays built by the local wheelwright. Messrs Crowley & Co. of Alton in Hampshire followed this path for many years, buying their drays from Thornycroft who were located at Basingstoke, a mere 12 miles away. The brewers themselves served their local areas, and often business was done on a personal basis, with the proprietors of both vendor and purchaser making the deal at the highest level.

Above: In common with many other brewers, Everard's of Leicester were users of Sentinel steam wagons. This copy of an old photograph shows that the three main chassis types were favoured, namely four wheeler and trailer, rigid sixwheel and articulated outfit. The scene is staged outside the Southgate Brewery. It is interesting to note that the older Standard type Sentinels have high slatted side bodies, while the later DG models employ chains beneath a substantial nameboard. The heavily riveted semi-trailer is also a Sentinel product.

Different approaches to publicity and vehicle lettering is displayed in these two photographs of Thornycroft A3 models of 1929 (right) and 1930 (far right). The very plain high-sided vehicle is in service with Noakes & Co Ltd of Black Eagle Brewery, Bermondsey and shows the very minimum of lettering to publicise its owners, or perhaps it is actually owned by a contractor. The other displays a livery and lettering style much more in keeping with the period, and which was used by Child & Co, a firm of contract bottlers operating from Leicester Square.

Above: This high, open-sided body was widely used in the brewing industry because it allowed mixed loads to be carried without the necessity for sheets and ropes to retain the load. Where several deliveries were made en route, it also allowed for load sorting and the stacking of empties without any risk of them falling off at the first roundabout! This fine old Thornycroft of Tamplins of Brighton has a loose tilt cover to ward off the rain in winter, and the sun during the summer. The problems associated with having a vehicle tailboard as large as this is evident when loading from a bank. The tailboard has to be lowered before the vehicle backs up, and then there is the danger of it being damaged. Usually a small gap is left, just wide enough to be dangerous to the loaders, so a board is placed to enable crated loads to be wheeled in on sack trucks.

Photographed at Leyland just prior to delivery, is this impressive TQ1 'Buffalo' for Ashby's Staines Brewery Ltd, a local family brewery with trade in the immediate area. Dating from 1930 this 6-ton machine was of 16ft. 9in. wheelbase and was carried on 38"x8" tyres. The massive 55hp petrol engine was started by means of the fixed starting handle, and assistance in bringing the vehicle to rest was by means of the auxiliary servo, seen just above the nearside cab step. Access to the load on this high sided body is by means of five hinged drop-sections, and facility for easy lowering is provided by the steel bars secured on the side hinges

Right: It is half-past-eight, and the four Thornycrofts of Barclay Perkins and Co. have been loaded and now their drawbar trailers have been coupled and reversed onto the bank for their load of casks. An official Thornycroft photograph of around 1933, it is far more interesting than the usual 'posed against a fence' type of photo which manufacturers normally adopt. The small cranes positioned at the back of the loading bank are unusual, these could have been used to load a vehicle positioned away from the bank or to handle butts or hogsheads that were considered too heavy and dangerous to be manhandled into position.

Right: Beautifully turned out in the Bass livery of the period, this 1931 model JO6 Garner is carefully posed outside the builder's premises in Birmingham prior to delivery. Being registered in Brighton, it could well have been a vehicle belonging to a local haulage contractor, rather than the brewery itself. Bass used the railways as their main carrier, leaving actual deliveries in the hands of local road hauliers.

Pictured outside the old Ponders End, Enfield works of the Arlington Motor Company, is this 1934 Leyland 'Cub' destined for the Cambridge brewery of Greene, King Ltd. The 'Cub' models were widely used by breweries at the lighter end of their delivery fleets, often replacing the older and larger Leylands operated by many of them. This was the medium weight Leyland of the 'thirties, aimed at beating off competition from the likes of Bedford, Commer and Ford as well as some of the US imports of the period.

Right: One of the problems facing brewery delivery crews is the unfailing interest of small children, when they see the barrels of beer being solemnly lowered into public house cellars. Draymen have to be continually on the look-out for unwary pedestrians who might inadvertently step into the open cellar, and small children have been known to play chase around the waiting casks and forget all about the gaping abyss where there was once a pavement! Here we see a 1936 Leyland 'Cub' awaiting its load of empties while the draymen expertly handles the casks with his stout barrel rope. Nice period touch is the fixed starting handle on the 'Cub', but the driver must have had a problem seeing through that nearside window, which has been replaced by an opening hatch!

Below: Nicholson and Sons of Maidenhead, Berks. were one of the brewers who favoured the use of a full box van, as shown by this mid 1903s AEC 'Matador'. It probably has a tailboard and shutter or curtains at the rear, while side access for unloading was through double doors in the centre, which had a stout bar beneath for the barrel slide or crate slide. Bodywork was by Normand of Park Royal. Note the large autovac on the nearside cab quarter panel which acted as a fuel feed to the engine in place of the lift pump of later days. Nicholsons passed into the hands of Courage and Barclay at the end of the 1950s.

Below right: It is not clear from this photograph what type of load was carried on this Commer mediumweight for William Hancock & Co of Cardiff, for it has a very small headboard and a tiny side rave, and a decided absence of ropehooks for load security. Perhaps it was not fully fitted out when photographed inside the Luton works of Commer Cars, with a white sheet tied up to hide any production machinery. Note the style of cab fitted to this N4 model has the forward opening doors, which could prove very dangerous in use.

A nice working shot of this war-time Dennis 'Max' in service with Meux & Co. of London, shows how mixed loads of cask and bottled beer were often handled by the crew. The low-sided body has drop-sides only at the front section where the crated beer is off-loaded, the casks being stacked at the rear and off-loaded at the back of the vehicle. This style of body has no tailboard, the load being retained by a couple of steel rods, seen lying beneath the vehicle. The scene is Hornsey Rise, Islington in May 1952.

A diminutive Scammell 'Mechanical Horse' artic makes a delivery to a local house in this Friary publicity photograph. As though frozen in time, the drayman holds a firkin steady on the barrel skid which appears to be almost as long as the tiny trailer, while the publican — or his cellarman — scrutinises the delivery notes and prepare to flick the ash from his filter cigarette. The sheet has been nonchalantly thrown back, to reveal part of the load which includes pints and flagons, various casks, and probably some empties on the pavement. Note the chunky 3.5 inch letters on the registration plate which have been carefully separated by full stops — just as illegal as the use of variable spacing and bolt heads by some poseurs on cars of today.

This evocative photograph of William Younger's vehicles at the empty cask shed
at one of their Edinburgh breweries, was probably taken around 1937,
showing as it does the Morris-Commercial 'Leader' at right. The Leylands are
older, the first two are both 1930 machines, that in front registered in
Edinburgh, whilst the second bears a London registration of the same year. The
far vehicle dates from the late twenties.

Left: Supplying the public directly through their own public houses, the brewers have always sought to publicise their products by way of sales drives, sponsorships and carnival processions, often using their own vehicles. This trio of Guys — two 'Vixens' and a 'Wolf', formed the entry for Cobb's Margate Brewery in the 1947 Broadstairs Carnival, and one of the Vixens took first prize. Bodywork and painting of the vehicles was carried out by Hayward Brothers of Whitstable, Kent. Cobb & Co. passed to Whitbreads in 1968 and was promptly closed down.

Below: Aimed at local and home trade, Davenports of Birmingham turned to electric vehicles as quiet, efficient means of transport for light loads over short distances. This Morrison Electric, built in 1947, retains the dairy float image for the cab portion, but the load carrying part has been tastefully enlarged with a smooth raised panel to make the transition less obtrusive. A large rear panel is provided for added publicity, and the traction batteries are accessible for recharging via hinged panels on the nearside, below the body floor.

Left: With just a few cartons of Carlsberg on the trailer, this export version of the Scammell 'Scarab' is posed outside the 'Artichoke' not far from the Scammell plant at Watford. The outfit was destined for the Scammell stand at the International Commercial Motor Show at Earls Court in 1948, and formed part of an order for the Danish brewery for local deliveries around Copenhagen.

In the days preceding World War II it was unusual to find Fords among the ranks of brewery vehicles. In the old days of 'three on the floor' gearboxes, 6volt electrics and vacuum wipers, Fords were a rarity in brewery fleets, and it was not until the range became more orthodox, that the marque made any serious inroads into the trade. This 1956 edition of the Thames ET6 model with a 4D Ford diesel engine, was one of a handful operated by Meux & Co. from their Nine Elms brewery.

Typical of the everyday problems facing retail delivery drivers is this scene of a house delivery being made in High Street, Hampton, in April 1957. The Dennis 'Pax' of Watneys has come from the nearby Mortlake brewery with a load of small casks, typical of the off peak orders of many of the smaller public houses — 10gallons, pins and firkins. Whilst the crew are busying themselves with opening up the cellar flap and preparing the delivery, a Union Cartage driver is forced to take to the pavement in order to negotiate the parked brewers dray — only to fall foul of the projecting shop blind at right — all in a day's work!

Although a posed publicity photograph for the newly introduced Commer forward control chassis, this shot is interesting for its inclusion of draymen. A large dumping pad is being used here for the unloading of some 36 gallon casks, which are, in all probability, empty on this occasion. Two of the crew have the leather aprons normally used by the trouncers, and it could be that the third man is the driver. A nice touch is the carefully scalloped body headboard which is presumably to give the driver better rearward vision, but on this new vehicle no nearside mirror has been fitted!

In the period following World War II, one vehicle which typified the local delivery brewers dray was undoubtedly the Dennis 'Pax'. Available originally with the makers own petrol engine, a diesel engine option was offered later. With a wheelbase of 3.5m. and a set-back front axle, it was a plain vehicle built to the highest standards by a very old established lorry manufacturer, a company which in many ways was typical of the brewing industry itself. This example was one of some 130 supplied to Watneys, and in this instance carries a modern all-metal body supplied by Tubular Metal Bodies, an associate company of J. H. Sparshatt.

A familiar sight in the 1950s were the Leylands of Magee Marshall & Co. of Bolton, and they operated quite a number of 'Comet' rigids with drawbar trailers. The summer trade in holiday towns such as Blackpool, is a healthy one for the brewers, particularly during the factory holidays or 'wakes weeks' when hotel accommodation is at a premium. Hence the need for drawbar trailers to handle the tremendous surge in trade. Some of the Magee 'Comet' outfits were originally supplied with petrol engines, and these were later converted to oilers.

Although the Commer name had been borne by vehicles with payloads of up to 10 tons in pre-war days, the advent of the 'underfloor' 5 ton model in 1948 gave added stature to the marque. Many operators who had never run a Commer in their fleet were so impressed by the machine that orders came rolling in. The addition of the two-stroke TS3 engine to the range in 1950 provided additional popularity which resulted in articulated models and even drawbar types being added to the range. The photograph above shows a 5-ton diesel engined model delivered to Flowers Breweries of Luton in 1955, while left is quite a rare 1948 trailer model in service with H & G Simonds on Reading, and used with a diminutive tank trailer.

Some of the most attractive Leylands were undoubtedly the 'Steer' models, with their twin steering front axles. This 15S machine was just one of 60 Leylands operated by Ansells Brewery Ltd of Aston, Birmingham during the 1950s. Body length was 20ft 6in which provided space for 245 two-dozen cases of bottled beer or for 24 hogsheads plus 14 smaller casks on top, as shown here.

It is only in comparatively recent times that lagers have enjoyed such wide popularity amongst drinkers in this country, but there have always been some who preferred the particular brewing style, and some brewers who served the market. The Wrexham Lager Beer Company took over an older establishment in 1900 and continued to brew the particular beer through several changes of control and ownership. In 1948 this underfloor engined Commer must have been one of the first in service, for that was the year the revolutionary model Commer was introduced. Note the absence of any barrels on this neat load, for the demand for lager was slight compared to that for ales and stout. The lidded crates are also of special design and one wonders how they functioned on the conveyers along the bottling line.

The post-war delivery fleet of Flowers & Sons of Stratford Upon Avon included a number of Foden and Maudslay four wheelers. As they were replaced in the late 1950s the choice swung toward AEC, probably because of the ACV involvement. This ACV publicity photograph was arranged with one of the batch of 'Mercurys' being posed outside one of the houses with which the area has become connected. The deep sides on the body are typical of the fleet, and this was the period when many brewers thought a platform body with ropes and sheet adequate for load security. Whoever designed the headboard obviously did not seem to care about the aerodynamics of the vehicle!

Leyland publicity photograph to illustrate how Watneys had installed a crew cab on some of their 12B 'Beaver' delivery vehicles, which were used with drawbar trailers on some of the longer delivery runs which necessitated a night out. Light alloy body and crew cab by Sparshatts Metal Bodies.

The vehicle illustrated left is one of a similar large number supplied to Courage & Barclay. So many leading brewers used Dennis vehicles in this period, that the company was able to publicise the fact by using an advertisement which displayed many of the brewery trade marks of the day. The heavier 'Max' and 'Jubilant' also numbered among many brewery fleets, but it was the 3-ton and 5-ton 'Pax' models which formed the basis of this long association between vehicle builder and users in one industry.

BEER AT 3ft 2⅜ins

The vehicle shown is a low loader built for Whitbread upon a Dennis chassis with a laden height from ground to floor top of 3' 2⅜", when on 9.00 x 20 tyres.

Specialized body building is something in which the Body Building Division of Dennis Brothers have had years of experience. Work is undertaken upon single vehicles or fleets of vehicles, the hand built body being fitted to the chassis of the customers own choice, and including any special fitments.

 Body Building Division
Dennis Brothers Ltd., Guildford

Left: Probably more than any other industry, the breweries have for many years striven to achieve lower and safer loading for their vehicles. The original loading height was around four feet, no doubt brought about by the height of old horsedrawn carts and loading banks. With the advent of palletisation, there was no reason to maintain such a high floor line and labour representatives were always urging the brewers to reduce it as far as possible. One way in which Whitbreads tackled the problem was to get Dennis Brothers to produce bodywork which was attached to the chassis side members without the conventional longitudinal body runners. But in order to maintain an adequate carrying capacity 9.00x20 tyres had to be used, hence the need to provide the wheel boxes over the rear wheels. The possibilities of front wheel drive had been considered, but rejected because of high cost and loss of manoeuvrability. This contemporary Dennis advertisement proclaims the loading height achieved at that time.

Right: During the late 1950s, Wilsons Brewery of Newton Heath, Manchester, took delivery of a number of these bonnetted ERF delivery vehicles, specially designed so as to allow for three men to be accommodated in the cab, something impossible with the regular forward control cab designs of the day. Some of their earlier vehicles had been Sentinels, and their cabs did allow for three crew members, because of the underfloor engine layout.

Left: This late 1956 model Albion 'Claymore' 5-tonner was in service in Edinburgh with William Younger & Co, and is pictured handling a load of empty barrels at the empties bank. With its underfloor engine layout, the 'Claymore' allowed for a three-seater cab which was positioned low down and well forward of the front axle. Engine accessibility was similar to that of the Sentinel, but with such a short wheelbase most of the inter-axle space was taken up with the engine/gearbox combination.

One of the experimental types of delivery vehicle put into service by Mitchells & Butlers at their Cape Hill brewery in Birmingham, was this variation of the Albion 'Reiver' chassis. By adding another axle and using just 16 inch wheels it was possible to provide a long, low body, capable of carrying 10-tons, yet allowing plenty of space for the delivery crew to be able to sort the load and segregate the empties en route. One rather old style feature of the vehicle was the positioning of wipers on the headboard!

For the major part of its transport, Bass & Co relied heavily upon the railways up to the 1960s. Wagon-loads of cask beer would be dispatched from the Burton-upon-Trent brewery to depots throughout the country, where it would be distributed either by the local railway depot transport or by hired road transport contractors. In the London area, St. Pancras Station was the focal point for the trade, and a large warehouse was given over to beer storage with conditioning cellars. The actual deliveries were handled by the United Service Transport who operated a fleet of vehicles complete in Bass Worthington colours, and this Bedford S-type artic was just one of the fleet used.

Posing for the camera just after being painted and before
the windscreen wipers were fitted (!), this Guy 'Otter'
was destined for service with Greenall, Whitley & Co.
Delivered as a chassis/scuttle, a larger than standard cab
was built for the delivery crew by Holmes of Preston,
who also provided the platform body complete with
stanchions and rubber-covered chains. Unusual is the
white painted cab roof which has headboards facing fore
and aft. Even the inside of the body is finished in white.

Austin commercials were not so widely used in brewery
fleets as the Bedfords, but the 3-, 5- and 7-ton models
were quite well represented in different parts of the
country. This late 1959 model 5KWE was one of several
in the Charringtons fleet which embodied plain dropside
bodywork in preference to special delivery body styling.

Left: It is only natural that brewers located north of the border in Scotland should support their local vehicle builder, and Archibald Campbell, Hope and King of Edinburgh were no exception. This mid-1960s Albion 'Chieftain' Super Six is a long wheelbase model and carries a plain platform body which renders the load net very necessary. Pictured on delivery work in Glasgow the crew are down to just a few casks, even though the long shadows signify it is still early morning.

Right: Highly unusual in any delivery sphere, the introduction of rigid eight wheel BMC chassis to the Mitchells and Butlers division of Bass Charrington in 1970, was a move to maximise loading space and vehicle capacity. Each of the 12 LR1000 model BMC 'Laird' four wheel chassis was converted to four axles by Primrose Third Axle Co. Ltd who used identical BMC axles as those originally fitted. The chassis was also lengthened and strengthened as required. Bodywork was by Burton and Coles and its quick-release side bars gave all round load access. The gross weight was 16.5 tons which provided a payload of 10 tons on the 24ft 6in long body.

Left: Lorimer's Breweries Ltd of Edinburgh added four Ford D-series artics to their delivery fleet in 1979, and these were the first of the urban delivery articulated type fitted with Boalloy Tautliner bodies. These D1611 units were similar to the D1610 but had the Dorset 6.2 litre diesel engine in place of the standard 6 litre power unit. Operating at 16 tons gcw, the outfits were used for deliveries to houses in southern Scotland, and the six speed fully synchromesh gearbox was specified in an effort to maintain adequate performance in spite of a mediocre power to weight ratio.

Right: The early 1970s saw a profusion of twinsteering six wheelers on the brewery scene, as transport managers attempted to obtain large loading platforms at a reasonable loading height, yet managing to load the vehicle to somewhere near its design capacity without resorting to dangerously high load stacking. The TK Bedford type was the most popular, with the D-series Ford following. More unusual was the Leyland mediumweight variation in the shape of the 'Laird', seen here in service with Josua Tetley of Leeds.

Left: Following upon their successes with four wheel, six wheel and twin steer versions of their TK model, Bedford were also the leaders in supplying a specially designed low-frame tractor unit for the 'Urban Artic' concept of the 1970s. This design of trailer, with its removable posts and bars, is adaptable for use as a hand-loaded local delivery vehicle, or as a fork-truck loaded bulk load carrier for palletised loads.

Right: During its long civilian production run from 1960 to 1984 the TK Bedford was widely used in the brewing industry in a variety of uses. The rigid chassis models formed the basis for many local delivery vehicles, and the articulated tractors found a niche in the market with the high capacity urban delivery type. This 1977 model in service with Davenports is seen coupled to a flat semi-trailer fitted with detachable metal side panels for easy access to any part of the load.

Left: Urban Delivery — 1980s Style. Several of the large brewing groups took to equipping their fleet with the Dodge 'Commando' rigids during the 1980s, and to stacking the loads higher in order to achieve full capacity. This Boalloy-bodied example employs the manufacturers curtain-sided design at the rear as well as both sides, and every curtain is load-bearing with tension applied both horizontally and vertically.

Left: The Yorkshire brewery firm of Webster's celebrated 150 years of service in 1988, and as if to mark the occasion work on a new distribution centre at Elland near Halifax began in November of that year. Within 28 weeks the new centre was opened and was equipped with 30 Volvo FL6.17 local delivery vehicles. These modern editions of brewery drays incorporate some of the latest technology which includes air suspension with loadheight control and on-board computer linked with the brewery barrel bar coding system. Operating at 17tonne gross, the Volvos are fitted with the makers 207bhp engine.

Early in 1970 Whitbreads started experiments with a drawbar trailer combination which embodied a two wheel dolly with fifth wheel turntable to support the front of the trailer. The theory behind the design was to load both vehicle and trailer for deliveries in a particular area, and to permanently locate a tractor unit somewhere convenient to the delivery round. The outfit would rendezvous with the tractor unit, uncoupling the trailer as a semi-trailer and proceed on its deliveries. The tractor unit picking up the semi and proceeding to another area for its delivery round. At the end of the day the two vehicles would again meet at a predetermined point and change the (semi) trailer over, with the combination then returning to the depot. In the two photographs to the left the vehicle is pictured as a complete drawbar combination, as two separate outfits and in the picture above designer Gordon Goddard can be seen carefully watching the outfit being jackknifed on its first run. He was also responsible for much work in connection with the setting up of BTAC — the informal association of Brewery transport managers. The photograph to the right shows a larger version of the concept, this time based on an experimental sixwheel Scammell 'Trunker'.

Above: During the 1980s the Phoenix brewery Co. of Brighton acquired a fleet of Dodge drop frame chassis, together with a greater number of Ray Smith demountable bodies which incorporated Boalloy Localiner bodywork. This photograph shows the front support legs being extended in preparation for driving away the chassis/cab to leave the body section standing on its four legs, as those in the background. The body design incorporates sliding panel sections and folding curtains at the sides, with a rolling shutter at the rear; the webbing straps are for load restraint. Note that there is a specially strengthened section over the rear axle, which provides extra rigidity and support for the roof. Because of the low floor line, low wheelboxes have had to be provided for the rear wheels — in this instance 10gallon kegs are stacked there.

Right: In recent years the AWD marque has tried valiantly to cling on to the considerable share of the brewery delivery trade, which its predecessor Bedford did so much to establish. Latest trend is for the 'Urban Artic' style which tried to combine the features of low-loading, load security and vehicle manoeuvrability. The first of these features is achieved by running on low-profile tyres of adequate section, the second by utilising the reinforced style of tensioned side curtains and the third by using a powerful short wheelbase tractor unit. This AWD TL21-16 for Mansfield Brewery is designed for a gcw of 21tons, and is fitted with the Perkins Phaser turbocharged 160bhp engine. The design has been developed from the successful TL1930 — low load — concept. In this instance a tandem axle trailer forms the combination, unusual in the Urban Artic sphere.

When Britains last remaining heavy vehicle builder ERF, announced that it was going to use the Steyr cab for its new range in 1989, many pundits thought it a retrograde step for the revered maker. But the brewery trade seems to like it and it is good to see a reversal of the trend toward imported vehicles. As for the cab, well, economics play their part, and if a suitable cab can be obtained, why not buy it instead of tooling up yourself? This version of the model follows the trend of painting vehicles to advertise a particular brand name rather than letter the vehicle with the title of the brewery.

LONG DISTANCE VEHICLES

The long distance transport of beer is nothing new, British beer was sent to the colonies way back in steamship days, and several brewers used to send beer by train to distant customers.

Our interest lies in the road transport fleets, and in this respect long distance carrying probably dates from the 1920s, and probably carried out by hauliers rather than own vehicles, although there are reports of long distance deliveries by steam wagons during that era.

The function of moving beer in casks, kegs, bottles or cans as opposed to in bulk, is primarily to serve a customer in a location where the brewer has no local distribution facility, or to stock a remote distribution depot. The circumstances can vary however, and the line of demarcation between a 'local' delivery and a 'trunk' delivery can become blurred. On some widespread delivery rounds it is necessary to use a maximum capacity vehicle and take two days for the round trip. On other occasions part of the load may be for the provincial depot and the balance for one big customer en route — the variations are numerous.

The more simple arrangement is that the brewery produces the beer and despatches it in bulk tanks to the bottling/canning plant. Here it is decanted into the small containers arranged on pallets and despatched on to a transfer vehicle to the distribution depot. Here it is sorted into loads, repalletised and sent on to the customer on local delivery vehicles. Similarly the cask/keg beer might be racked directly into containers at the brewery and despatched on the transfer vehicle or the casks/kegs could be filled at the production depot which fills the bottles and cans.

So the trunk/long distance/transfer vehicle could be carrying full loads of casks, kegs, bottles or cans or any permutation to suit the demands of the particular distribution depot. This can vary enormously from place to place and at the various seasons and peaks during the year. Added to this there is the small demountable tank for bulk deliveries to cellars, which are sometimes carried long distances to service particular customers.

Vehicles design has naturally included rigids, drawbars and articulated types, the lorry and drawbars of the fifties now having been replaced by the artic, which in turn now finds itself being ousted by the new breed of drawbar combinations finding increased use in large fleets.

Body types used for long distance work varied little for many years, the ubiquitous flat with sheets and ropes holding centre stage for a very long time. Sided and slatted vehicle bodywork has been favoured by some although palletisation favours an uncluttered body side. As with the local delivery types, the curtainsider has achieved some following, particularly after the spectacular displays of vehicle handling at M.I.R.A. at Nuneaton, when engineers tried their hardest to eject palletised beer kegs from a fast cornering artic!

Pictured alongside the allotments in Tolpits Lane opposite the Scammell factory, this resplendent articulated sixwheeler for Strong & Co. of Romsey, Hampshire, illustrates the huge bodies possible by using the Scammell design. The chain-driven tractor has the modern electric lighting and a proper cab with double opening windscreen, and the high sided trailer is strongly built to withstand the movement of heavy cask loads over the indifferent roads of the day. The characteristic bow front to the trailer gives the greatest floor area possible and the front and rear ends are tied by the imposing side nameboards. Three openings per side are provided for access to the load, the two rearmost having a strong bar at floor level for attaching the barrel skid with is stowed just below the floor on the nearside.

46 Brewery Transport

Left: Witnessing the huge success of the Scammell articulated heavyweights, several manufacturers tried to secure a share of the market by producing similar designs. The Carrimore-Lynx was one such production which achieved considerable success for its builders Carrosserie Latymer, a trailer builder with French origins and which later became Carrimore Trailers and then Anthony Carrimore. The name Carrimore was coined to impart just what the name said, and the Lynx part was a play on the word 'links' to mean articulated.

Below left: The old labour-intensive system of hand-loading is evident in this photograph, which shows three men handling a load of pint and quart crates on a Mark II AEC 'Mammoth Major' of Whitbread & Co. These AECs carried loads of bottled beer to the company's provincial depots at Leicester, Birmingham, Bristol, Norwich, Brighton etc.

Above: It is a great pity that the background of this early Scammell photo has been carefully removed in order to give more emphasis to the vehicle, for we are left with a tantalising foreground of railway tracks, sleepers and cobbles. Probably taken in the railway yard adjacent to the brewery, the re-toucher has painstakingly picked out the chains on the body, but then carefully removed the offside section to the rear of the cab! Several brewers turned to the Scammell in the 1920s because of the huge body space presented by the adoption of the articulated principle.

Below: Carefully posed beneath the clock of Chiswick Bottling Stores, this 1931 articulated eight wheeler was the first of a new batch of Scammells on contract from General Roadways to Whitbreads. Boasting a 14ton payload and carried at a speed of 16-18 mph, the outfit returned a fuel consumption of 5mpg according to the Scammell literature of the day. Note, however, that in true haulier manner, even the tailboard has to be used when transporting pint crates. Another virtue extolled in the brochure was that by running on large section singles, there was no chance of overloading the tyres as could happen with twins on an uneven road.

George Younger & Son Ltd of Alloa were long-time users of Thornycrofts for some reason, and in 1948 added this 'Trusty' to their fleet for long distance operation. Several brewers used nets for load security where a sheet was not required for load protection, as with this load of hogshead and barrels. It was rather different with wooden crates, because a net could get snagged on a rough edge or projecting staple and when the net was pulled off several boxes could come crashing down.

Below: Looking very much like a DG Foden cab, this style of Mark 3 'Mammoth Major' was unusual in the AEC fleet of Trumans. It was operated on the transfer of cask beers between their breweries in London and Burton-upon-Trent, and is pictured running into London with a load of hogshead of Burton Ale in 1955. The floor of the vehicle is covered by casks standing on their heads, and the second layer is loaded in the centre of the vehicle 'on the roll' but carefully scotched.

Right: Several times the long distance operation of brewery transport has been reported on in the trade press, and more than once Whitbreads have formed the subject of these articles. This evocative night time shot of a 1937 Scammell rigid eight was probably taken sometime in the late 1930s, for it is one of the fleet operated by C. D. & T. Contracts Ltd from their modern depot at Power Road, Chiswick. Although nationalised in 1950, the contract was continued in BRS days with a mixture of Scammell, Foden, AEC and Leyland eight wheelers. From the road signs in the photograph the location appears to be just outside Gloucester, and the vehicle was running between Chiswick and Cardiff with bottled beer.

Right: During the 1930s Pickfords managed a contract for Ind Coope & Allsopp which included a number of Bedford local delivery vehicles and this rather impressive AEC. At first sight a heavy sixwheeler of the 'Mammoth' range, closer inspection reveals that it is in fact a passenger chassis, and the radiator bears both 'Regal' and 'Oil Engine' scripts. The thinking behind the vehicle is not clear, for presumably a passenger chassis was considered for its low-loading layout, but in this instance the regular twin rears have been discarded in favour of giant singles on two axles. This feature has made it necessary to increase the height of the underbody longitudinal bearers substantially, thus bringing the body floor up to a height similar to that of a conventional lorry!

Below: With a brewery in Watford, Hertfordshire, it is not surprising that Benskins Watford Brewery did use a few Scammells in their fleet, if only for long distance work. This nice shot of a rigid eight in the brewery yard appears to be genuine, with a real mixed load of half-pints, pints, flagons and casks, all arranged in a not-too-particular manner. The high, steel framed body with post and wire inserts, seems well able to contain any combination of load, and the arched top tie-bars are a guard against bulging of the sides. The sheet was merely to prevent the rain washing off the bottle labels or the sun from warming up the beer too much. Note the railway track alongside the bank — a reminder of earlier days when the railways handled much of the long distance traffic of breweries throughout the country.

A fine load of hogshead, barrels and kilderkins is carried on this late 1940s Scammell R8 and trailer, operated from the Park Royal brewery by Thomas Allen Ltd. Note how load security is achieved with just a few strands of rope round the rearmost casks, and with the dumping pads wedged between the casks for a bit of extra grip. A wide variety of vehicles had been used on the Guinness contract, which had its origins in 1854. The arrangement continued after the opening of the Park Royal brewery in 1936, when Thomas Allen Ltd built a garage alongside the brewery as well as providing 28 houses for their drivers and mates.

This 1951 'Octopus' was averaging 9.5mph after being in service for a few months, according to the Leyland publicity of the period. It was also reported that Morgans of Norwich were well pleased with their 2201 'Octopus', for it had enabled a reduction in their delivery cost from 13/- (65p) to 9/- (45p) per ton to be made, against an unspecified predecessor.

Right: Probably the peak of British lorry style was reached in the mid 1950s with vehicles such as this 'Mammoth Major' in service with Whitbreads. For historical reasons, the Whitbread fleet was divided into two district categories — that for the breweries and another for the bottling depots. This state of affairs persisted until the early 1960s when the two fleets were amalgamated. Pictured outside the body builders premises in Kingston-upon-Thames, it is the epitome of the long distance brewery transport where everything is of the best quality and maintained to perfection. This vehicle has the traditional style of sided body with centre drop-sections, although loading was usually carried out from the rear. A high and substantial headboard provides stability for the load, which was protected by a fitted sheet secured by webbing straps which were carried down inside the body sides so as not to cover the company's name.

Above: In the days before the Carlsberg brewery was established at Northampton in 1970, supplies had to be imported from Denmark. This 10-ton Commer articulated outfit was one of several operated on behalf of the brewers by Thomas Allen Ltd., and is pictured at Ipswich docks after loading the consignment of cases. The tractor is powered by the makers famous two stroke TS3 diesel. Note the arrangement of exhaust silencers across the front of the vehicle, there was no room to mount them at the rear of the cab because of the short wheelbase.

Right: Finished in the pale primrose yellow of Flowers Breweries, this Thornycroft 'Trusty' PF model was powered by the makers own six cylinder oil engine of 7.88 litres capacity. Delivered to Flowers in September 1955 it was allocated to the Sunderland brewery which J. W. Green had acquired from George Younger & Sons Ltd in 1952. Flowers used Thornycroft, AEC and Sentinel heavy rigids for their trunk work before they decided to switch to artics in the early 1960s.

One of the Guinness fleet of Mark 5 'Mammoth Major' insulated vans specially built to take loads of draught containers, seen here being unloaded at Park Royal. While most brewers went for 5- and 10-gallon metal beer kegs, Guinness adopted a special 11-gallon keg for their trade, and to avoid problems with CO_2 supply also provided each container with its own integral gas cartridge within the cask. Early Draught Guinness vehicles were turned out in the overall blue livery, but the one depicted here is in the later cream bodywork colour. Note the railway tracks running alongside the loading bank, a reminder that in days gone-by much of the long-distance traffic in Guinness was handled by the railways, including the interesting road-rail tanks used before the advent of ISO containers.

The brewing industry was not a great user of the Dodge marque until after WWII, probably because of its American background. Since then the name has appeared on more vehicles in the industry, this continuing right through to the acquisition by Renault. Pictured here are a couple of Dodge '500' model articulated tractors, part of a large fleet operated by Ind Coope of Romford and Burton-on-Trent for depot transport work. Delivered in the mid 1960s, this pair are loaded with palletised 10-gallon kegs on their Scammell trailers. Note that each pallet of kegs is loaded alternately — i.e. three across then two sideways — thus ensuring that the pallets are tight up to each other for full use of body space as well as load security. The sheet is then securely tied down and then roped over every pallet.

Flanked by AECs, this KV-cabbed ERF was the Ind Coope entry for the Lorry Driver of the Year round held within the confines of the Southall works in 1965. A long-term user of ERFs, the Ind Coope fleet had just undergone a change in the late 1950s, when the old blue and gold livery had given way to this more modern cream and green with the DD logo of their much publicised Double Diamond Pale Ale. This double-drive six wheeler was used for inter-depot transfer work, and the type sometimes appeared with drawbar trailers.

As part of the up-dating of the long-distance fleet in the mid-1960s, Trumans added a batch of AEC 'Marshall' six wheelers. In this AEC photograph, an impressive load of empty new casks has been provided and a convenient local pub found for the background. In real life the load of kils would be securely roped at least!

An interesting trend of the 1980s was that of moving away from the heavyweight articulated vehicles, which had held sway as bulk load carriers for some 20 years, into the realms of close-coupled drawbar outfits. This modern design shows how the Allied Lyons brewery group see the future in 1990, for a vehicle of this type. An E8 model ERF with a Cummins 265 engine.

TANKERS

The earliest illustration noted of a beer tank shows a rectangular copper vessel of riveted construction, mounted on a horsedrawn vehicle, but that hardly represents the usual role of the tanker in brewery fleets.

With breweries having their roots in the past 200-300 years, they all started in a small way brewing their beers for local consumption with no need to transport their brews except to customers.

As a company grows larger either by expansion of sales area or through the acquisition of competitors, so the need to transport beer over longer distances becomes apparent. First this was done in the normal containers such as casks and bottles, but later the economics of using a bulk tank came into use.

Early tank designs used copper with the joints riveted and caulked, but these were heavy and so of small capacity. Mild steel was lighter and could be welded at the joints, but did not suit the brewers demands for cleanliness, so a glass lining was added. This feature demanded some form of flexibility and shock-absorbing mountings on the chassis in order to minimise the risk of fracture to the glass surface, which was difficult and expensive to repair, but it did provide an easily cleaned surface.

Aluminium and stainless steel had the attributes of low weight and hard surface respectively, but until comparatively recently there were problems with faultless welding.

Whatever material was used, it still needed to be insulated, for brewers are fussy when it comes to the condition of their beers, and it must not be allowed to get too hot, or too cold for that matter. Various types of insulation have been used over the years including cork, metal foil, mineral wool and glass fibre, over which had to be placed a sheathing to keep it in place, as well as providing a surface that could be used for advertising as well as looking good and clean!

As with the tank lining, the outer cladding has variously been riveted, screwed or butt-welded for appearance. Whereas the old glass-lined

Although not as popular as the 'Pax', the tractor versions of the type — named 'Horla' — was also used by some of the major brewers, although usually as articulated tractors. This Whitbread drawbar tractor is rather a hybrid, and was used in conjunction with 40barrel drawbar tanks which had originally been drawn by the unique Latil four wheel drive units. Note the neat panelled ballast box and nicely blackened spare wheels (one of each size for tractor and trailer) on this immaculate outfit photographed against the stark desolation of the London blitz in the background.

An interesting photograph of a dual-tank vehicle in its raw state before any lagging or shrouding was fitted. The caption describes it as being a 20-hogshead tank for Bass, Ratcliffe and Gretton, which means that they are a pair of 15-barrel vessels. Note how the two vessels are canted toward the centre of the vehicle in order to aid discharge of the contents, for the outlets are paired for ease of control. The vehicle appears to be of the 1930s, and the tanks are trunnion mounted to absorb some of the road shocks.

tanks required flexible mountings to the chassis, the modern stainless steel variety can be more rigidly mounted. Earlier designs used straps around the vessel, but later types embody mountings attached directly to rings around the tanks, and form fixings for the outer casing.

All tanks used to be cleaned by hand, hence the inter-external manway seen positioned along the tank side or in the dished end. This design allowed the manway door to be released when the tank was empty and be swung outward, providing just about enough space for a slim man to enter with his hosepipe and cleaning materials. The air/Co2 cock at the top of the tank would be opened for a bit of air, and the loading cock opened to release the dirty water. The more modern method is for in-place cleaning, which consists of suspending a sprinkler inside the tank through which a prepared cleaning fluid is pumped, thus removing the necessity for a man to enter the tank.

The earliest road tanks were of only 20 barrel capacity, but as demand has increased together with larger capacity vehicles being allowed, so tanks of 40-, 60-, 80-, 100- and 120-barrel size have come into use.

Tankers have been used on rigid vehicles, drawbar trailers, articulated trailers, as demountables, within an ISO container framework and as road/rail type vehicles. Some breweries have adopted several of these types during the same period, in order to maintain a certain degree of flexibility according to variations in trade. A trailer tank is less expensive to have idle than a rigid vehicle, while a demountable is even less so.

The drawbar or demountable also allows one vehicle to make two or more deliveries while on one journey, although a large vehicle with a compartmented tank, can perform a similar function. One drawback of using demountable tanks is that of having a suitable means of handling these, for whilst a fork

Below: Polished wooden barrels used on Watney tankers during the 1930-1960 period were a striking advertisement for the company, and in true brewery tradition they were even numbered among the normal barrel stock! In this photograph taken in the old Stag Brewery at Pimlico, the fleet of Scammell 'Scarab' artic tankers are on parade for some important visitors. The fleet of large 'wooden' tanks was not restricted to these artics, for they included rigid vehicles, drawbar trailers and some were demountables. Many of the tanks outlived their original chassis and were transferred to later undergear.

truck is able to handle small sizes, something like an ISO tank requires rather larger-scale equipment.

The main use of the large tankers is to transport beer in bulk to a bottling plant or canning facility which is remote from the brewery. At the brewery the beer is transferred to the road tank, usually under pressure from Co2, and often a back pressure of Co2 is attached to the top of the tanker to keep down the head of the beer and so prevent unnecessary foaming or 'fobbing' as it is termed. At the receiving point a greater pressure of Co2 will be applied to the top of the tanker, so pushing the beer out of the bottom cock which was used for filling. This method is also used should beer have to be transferred from one tanker to another at the roadside in cases of accident or breakdown, although it takes a very long time!

With the gradual increase in the use of beer storage tanks in house cellars, there has been a greater demand for tankers to carry out the transport junction. Whilst some brewers use the smaller 2½-, 5-, 8-, or 10-barrel demountable tanks on a small local delivery sized vehicle, others have resorted to providing special vehicles which have a selection of tanks permanently fixed on them. Yet other brewers, having very large houses with a similarly high draught beer trade, use large capacity road tankers suitable equipped with hosereels and dispensing equipment.

Above: While one operative attends to the loading main at the rear of the tank, another attaches the vent pipe to the front compartment ready for loading. Pictured under the loading facility at Park Royal, one of the large fleet of Mark 3 'Mammoth Major' 80-barrel tanks is prepared to take on a load of the dark liquid.

Above: A scene in the brewery yard, as one of the British Railways road/rail tanks is loaded, ready for the Bedford drawbar tractor to take it to Camden goods depot, where it will be shunted aboard the special railway wagon for its journey to Glasgow. Several brewers, and indeed dairies as well, used the road/rail tank concept for the long distance transport of tankers. In this instance the tank is of 40-barrel capacity and was owned by the brewer, British Railways supplying the undergear, the road transport and of course, the rail wagon. In this photograph, taken at Whitbreads, the operative is drawing off his sample from the vent cock at the top of the tank. Loading is carried out at the rear by means of the white hose.

Below: Why a two man crew is posed with this Leyland 'Steer' is unclear, for it did not normally operate with a trailer. The vehicle was one of seven of this type operated by London brewers Watney, Combe Reid & Co. This particular machine was turned out in the brown and red of C. Hammerton & Co. of Stockwell, who were taken over by Watneys in 1952. It carries a pair of tanks of 30-barrel and 20-barrel capacity, and was used to transport bulk loads to bottling depots. There are no extra hoses or gauges which would suggest it was used on cellar tank work — so why the second man, or was it a case of two drivers in order to get back to the brewery without resorting to a night out? This was in the days of 20mph and an 11 hour driving day.

Above: The long advertising board carried atop this tanker shows how some brewers saw the need to assure their customers, that the beer carried in a steel tank was just as wholesome as that delivered in those wooden casks. This 1950 'Octopus' of Marston, Thompson & Evershed of Burton-on-Trent, was certainly smartly turned out, with an 80-barrel APV stainless steel tank made up of three compartments — probably 2x30-barrel and 1x20-barrel. With its profusion of pressure gauges, ladders and top pressure hoses, it is ready for cellar tank delivery work.

Above: During the post-war period, AECs did good business supplying considerable numbers of their 'Mammoth Major' chassis to brewers. They appeared with flat bodies for carrying casks and bottled beer, and, as here, as tankers for bulk beer transport. The maximum capacity tank possible within the gross laden weight regulations of the period was 80 barrels (2880 gallons), and this was quite useful, for many brewery storage tanks were of similar capacity. In order to carry a variety of beers, some tanks were of two compartments as this example for Trumans. Tanks were made without any interior baffles as they would make cleaning difficult.

Right: A sight not often witnessed, this view of the tank loading dock at Park Royal shows a variety of rigid and articulated tanks being filled. The only registration number visible indicates fleet number 216, a 1960 AEC Mark V rigid eight. The variety of Guinness advertisements on the dished ends of the tanks is interesting, and the arrangement of the twin overhead loading mains is far more tidy than the methods used by some brewers.

Below: By the 1960s many brewers had realised the economy and convenience of installing cellar tanks, in place of the large numbers of individual casks used at some of the major outlets. The installations in house cellars were of 2.5-barrels upwards, and the vehicles used to supply the houses were usually of 20- to 30-barrels capacity, but for houses with a large draught trade, Bass, Mitchels & Butlers took to using maximum capacity artics! In this instance the driver is seen preparing the hoses prior to making a delivery to this house alongside Kings Cross Station in June 1965.

Right: The Seddon marque provided some popular vehicles during its lifespan, with the original oil-engine 6tonner being the best remembered. It was also responsible for some rather unusual and less popular models, such as the three-cylinder engined 25cwt, the Mk12 8tonner and the 'Sirdar' an 80ton gvw unit, these all being of the bonnetted variety. Almost as rare in the home market was the Mark 14, a 14ton gvw four wheel rigid also available as a tractor unit of 8ft.6in. wheelbase. Pictured here are the two Mark 14 rigid tankers operated by Whitbreads being unloaded at the Grays Inn Road bottling depot. At peak times these vehicles were used with drawbar trailers and occasionally could be seen on deliveries to provincial bottling plants.

Left: Pictured in the yard at Park Royal are five of a batch of 12 Mark 3 'Mammoth Major' tankers taken into service in 1957. Finished in the period livery of dark blue with gold harp and cream lettering, the vehicles have Duramin light alloy cabs and four-compartment 80-barrel tanks by Burnett & Rolfe of Rochester.

Above: Watneys early vehicles for bulk beer delivery were completed with the famous wooden cladding which gave the stainless steel tanks the appearance of extra large beer barrels. By the 1960s replacement vehicles were much more mundane affairs as shown by this Austin FF-series rigid fitted with a row of three 5-barrel tanks. The hinged side panels form covers for the outlet cocks on the nearside, as well as providing storage space for the tools and fittings necessary to carry out the deliveries.

Right: A fine example of a British brewery tanker of the 1960s, is this Gardner-engined Atkinson in service with the Bass Worthington organisation. The 80 barrel stainless steel tank is of the two compartment type with the inter-external mainways located on the nearside, as also are the two loading/unloading cocks. The small diameter pipes leading down from the top of the tank are to draw off the 'fob' during loading, and to apply CO_2 top pressure when unloading. Note that this vehicle is fitted with a front drawbar hitch for shunting trailer in depots, for often another tank or a cask beer trailer was added on depot journeys.

Above: The post-war years saw many brewers trying to increase their market share by entering into reciprocal trading agreements with brewers in other areas. By adding more 'brews' or 'labels' to their own, they are able to offer additional variety in their houses without actually having to vary their brewing programme. This was particularly useful in holiday areas where customers often sought out their regular local brew even when away from home, and many of the major breweries took advantage of this trend. In the 1960s Charringtons brewery actively marketed their Jubilee Stout in other areas, and this Foden S21 tanker has just unloaded at the nearby Mile End brewery and will soon be heading northwards back home to Sheffield.

Below: One of the most attractive of all brewery vehicles must be the twin steer ERF tankers operated by Scottish & Newcastle Breweries Ltd. Many ERFs were employed in the long distance fleet in both tanker and platform types, of both twinsteer and eightwheel arrangements. The LV-cabbed twinsteer carries a double compartment tank of around 60 barrels capacity, and has racks along both sides of the tank for displaying advertising boards.

Below right: The twinsteer chassis of the Bedford TK range was used by quite a number of brewery companies for local delivery work in the 1960s and 1970s. Not so widely used were bulk beer dispensing outfits like this example for the Burtonwood Brewery Co. which has four stainless steel tanks which are neatly manifolded to the dispensing hose at the rear. Side protection is by sliding plastic curtaining and the hosereel, metering equipment and outlet cocks are accessible under the large rear door.

Although perhaps not so obvious as the delivery vehicles, most brewery companies employ a small selection of miscellaneous vehicles for handling many of the ancillary tasks connected with the industry.

The building department might want the use of a general lorry for carrying out maintenance work on the public houses owned by the company for instance. Or the brewery might use a tipper for getting rid of builders rubbish, spent hops, boiler fuel or moving stores around the yard and buildings.

In small companies the wine and spirits department had the exclusive use of a van for their own deliveries if not forming part of the general delivery schedule. Some of the larger off-licensed premises might have a small van for deliveries which would be provided by the owning brewery and be maintained by them.

At least one brewery used to supply a vehicle for use by its sports club while in another an old van was used to tow the gang mower for the cricket and football fields. One or two of the larger horse-owning brewery companies kept a horsebox for use in moving the horses around to shows, while the dray was moved on a delivery vehicle.

The introduction of new methods in house cellar beer storage, has meant that maintenance crews have to be mobile in order to service the cooling equipment promptly. In the old days of wooden casks a reported leaking cask meant that a cooper was dispatched with his tools on his bike or on the bus!

The increase in awareness concerning publicity and advertising has meant providing vehicles to deliver, clean and service all manner of advertising signs, displays and equipment, while in some cases the brewers have gone to great expense in designing vehicles purely for advertising and we have seen vehicles disguised as barrels, crates and beer dispensers.

One other department that has always required the use of a non-delivery vehicle is the transport department or vehicle workshops, for they often have to go out to collect parts or to get a fitter out to a breakdown. Some companies resorted to keeping their own large breakdown vehicle for roadside recovery.

Not all brewery vehicles are immaculately turned out and used on delivery work. This 1950 O-type Bedford tipper was used as the building department tipper by James Hole & Co. of Newark on Trent, and in this role served as a service vehicle for clearing rubbish, carrying building materials, erecting pub signs and generally carrying anything other than beer. Most breweries of any size needed a vehicle of this type of handle the variety of tasks arising from running the brewery and servicing many tied houses.

Many brewers have their own wines and spirits departments which handle supplies to their houses and off-licences. In some cases deliveries are made on the same vehicle as that delivering the range of beers, but in others a separate delivery is made for a variety of reasons. In the mid 1930s Eldridge, Pope & Co. Ltd added this Commer 8cwt Super Van to their fleet, and it is pictured at the Luton works prior to delivery, after being painted in the customers livery, a service which was once carried out by the vehicle manufacturers.

Above: The natural progression for the delivery service of the corner off licence was from handcart and delivery bicycle to the small motor van. Truman's supplied this little 5cwt van for the use of the 'Little Brown Jug' at Wealdstone in Middlesex during the mid-1930s. Interesting to note that body sides, rear doors and cab doors are all adequately covered with advertising material. This is a 1935 model of the Morris Eight 5cwt van which at that time was sold at around £93!

Left: Long before the current craze of low alcohol beer there were a number of alternatives available for those who craved a non-alcoholic drink that wasn't a fizzy mineral water. Chandy was a less than two percent alcohol content drink created by the Chislehurst Mineral Water Company which passed into the Whitbread organisation, and one of their vehicles was this most unusual delivery van based on the Austin FX3 taxicab or hire car chassis of the mid 1950s.

Below: Although the Whitbread Shire horses were a very strong advertising feature, an additional form of publicity during the 1950s and 1960s was this display van based on the Austin 'Three-Way' chassis/front end. This was the period of heavy advertising for Mackeson Stout with efforts to make it available nationwide.

Many brewers have tried to impart a better image at outside events and functions by providing vehicle-based mobile bars. A rigid vehicle chassis puts the serving staff at too high a level, so the articulated outfit or drawbar trailer provides a much more convenient working height. This early fifties Bedford O-type articulated design was produced by Sparshatts of Portsmouth for local brewers Friary of Guildford.

Brewery transport managers often face the dilemma of whether to employ their own breakdown vehicle, or to call in professional recovery companies when they have a broken down vehicle at a remote location. Often the decision is taken by the accountants who argue that regular maintenance will reduce the chance of a breakdown, and that an own recovery vehicle standing idle is a drain of resources. The other side of the argument is that charges raised by outside garages for roadside recovery are often excessive and they have little respect for the vehicle or its load. This ex-local delivery vehicle in service with the vehicle maintenance department of Courage & Co. marks the compromise: if the vehicle is towable, then go and get it yourself; if it is a major accident or overturned vehicle, then call in the professionals.

Above: Many brewers had dispensed with horses for delivery work long before WWII, while others carried on until the 1950s with their role being gradually relegated to any very local work or mostly shows and carnival entries. Whitbreads have gained much publicity from their famous shires, and they underlined the fact that they had to work as well as appearing in shows and publicity events. This splendid Seddon-Carrimore articulated horsebox was added to the fleet in the 1950s, and the vehicle itself was almost as good a publicity media as the four horses it carried. Note that the vehicle even displays the names of the horses being carried — a feature which made no impression on the park-keeper at Hampstead Heath where it was photographed!

Above: The raw materials of beer brewing are basically hops, malted grain and lots of water, and many breweries were originally established where there was an ample supply of good quality water, and the other commodities could be brought in as required. Some brewers have their own hop growing farms, while some buy on the open market, and malt is sometimes obtained from specialist producers, as are other additives such as brewing sugars. Many brewers resort to collecting their supplies of malt grains in order to reduce the cost and have more control on the timing of deliveries, especially if there are problems with storage. This Dodge-hauled bulk malt carrier was one in service with Scottish & Newcastle Breweries during the 1960s.

Above: Before beers became so widely available from supermarkets, the take-home trade was served by off licences and wine merchants stores. Most of the larger shops could boast a delivery van of some kind, for bottled beer was heavy, especially in the days of old wooden crates, for these were the days before beer in cans was as popular as it is today. The Grapes at High Wycombe was unusual in having a 10-cwt Morris-Commercial J-type at their disposal, and the 150cu.ft. body made deliveries to the surrounding area easier than the more usual delivery vans based on private car running gear. However at 6ft.7in. high, plus that large headboard, most off licences could not accommodate anything so tall!

Above: In the old days with beer being delivered in either wooden casks or glass bottles, there was little need for any maintenance visits to public houses, save that of repairing the cellar flaps, hammering-up a leaking cask or perhaps unblocking the cellar drain. With the advent of pressurised metal casks, cellar storage tanks and beer coolers, the need for service personnel increased significantly. Many more small vans went into brewery use for the servicing of the equipment necessary to have the products in top condition. Based at the old Essex Brewery in Walthamstow was this little Commer 'Imp' van, which was used by the maintenance team of Tollemache & Cobbold in the late 1960s.

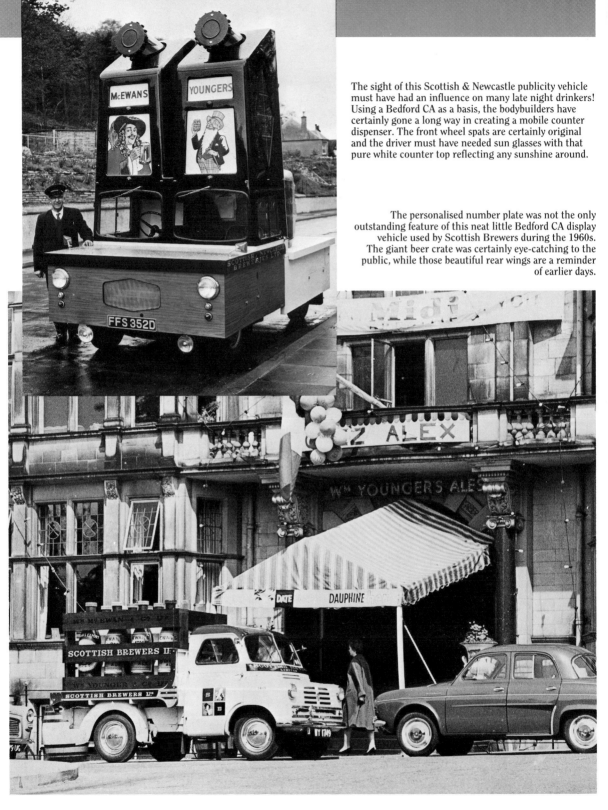

The sight of this Scottish & Newcastle publicity vehicle must have had an influence on many late night drinkers! Using a Bedford CA as a basis, the bodybuilders have certainly gone a long way in creating a mobile counter dispenser. The front wheel spats are certainly original and the driver must have needed sun glasses with that pure white counter top reflecting any sunshine around.

The personalised number plate was not the only outstanding feature of this neat little Bedford CA display vehicle used by Scottish Brewers during the 1960s. The giant beer crate was certainly eye-catching to the public, while those beautiful rear wings are a reminder of earlier days.